Math Play!

Diane McGowan & Mark Schrooten

Little Hands® is a registered trademark of Williamson Publishing.

Illustrations by Loretta Braren

WILLIAMSON PUBLISHING • CHARLOTTE, VERMONT

Little Hands®, *Kids Can!*®, and *Tales Alive!*® are
registered trademarks of Williamson Publishing
Company.

Kaleidoscope Kids™ is a trademark of Williamson
Publishing Company.

Library of Congress
Cataloging-in-Publication Data

McGowan, Diane, 1956-
   Math play!: 80 ways to count & learn/by Diane
McGowan & Mark Schrooten.
      p. cm. — (Little hands book)
   Includes index.
   ISBN 1-885593-08-2
   1. Counting. 2. Mathematics—Study and teaching
(Elementary)
   I. Schrooten, Mark, 1960- . II. Title. III. Series:
Williamson
   little hands book.
   QA113.M3936 1997   96-37806
   372.7044—dc21   CIP

Cover and interior design: Trezzo-Braren Studio
Illustrations: Loretta Trezzo
Printing: Capital City Press

Williamson Publishing Co.
P.O. Box 185
Charlotte, Vermont 05445
1-800-234-8791

Manufactured in Mexico

10 9 8 7 6 5 4 3 2 1

Dedication

To my husband Chuck, and
my children Wendy, Kim, and
Michael. Every day you add
to my happiness. Thanks
for your patience.
DM

To God and to the child
in each of us.
MS

Acknowledgments

We would like to thank Marjorie Cohen and the Childcare Center at Phoenix College for their helpful comments and encouragement. This book was made possible because of the dedication and support of the following people at Williamson Publishing: Jennifer Ingersoll, Susan and Jack Williamson, June Roelle, Judy Raven, and Jennifer Adkisson. Thanks also to Ken Braren and Loretta Trezzo Braren, whose creative illustrations animate each page of this book.

CONTENTS

Just for Kids

Take a walk around your home or school and look carefully at the things you see. What do you notice? That's right, there are numbers just about everywhere! You may see them on the face of a clock, on the door to your apartment, on the side of your cereal box, on your mailbox, even on the back of a friend's baseball shirt.

This book is full of many fun things to do with numbers — just wait until you get started! Some activities are better to do indoors, but there are plenty of others you can enjoy in the great outdoors. Best of all, you won't need to have extra people for the ideas to work, although inviting a few friends to play with you would be fun, too!

Get ready now, to discover patterns that are hiding everywhere, to count the birds and bugs you see each day, and to measure the milk or juice you drink during snacktime. Get ready to jump into some exciting math play!

Tips for the Grown-Ups

Watching children play is one of life's greatest pleasures. We believe early-learning math skills are best introduced to young children using playful activities that are brief, easy, and most importantly, fun. We wrote this book to help smooth the way for you along a path of discovery with a variety of active-learning experiences that encourage children's math readiness.

It's important that children are alert, happy, and in a playful mood when you introduce activities. Use whatever you are doing as an opportunity to play and learn about math, whether in the kitchen, at the store, or at the zoo. Each chapter introduces premath skills such as counting, recognizing numerals, measurement, shapes, and pattern recognition. All activities are nonthreatening and noncompetitive so that every child can experience early success. We've included math activities that are entertaining and create an atmosphere of playful learning and acceptance.

Children not only vary one from the other, but any one child changes day to day. Don't be surprised if a child seems to take "one step forward and two steps back" in pre-math skills. Simply start each play period at whatever point a child seems comfortable. This book is built with a lot of repetitive experiences and eventually a child will become comfortable with certain skills. If you don't become discouraged, your child won't either.

We have included some helpful hints with most activities. Use them whenever possible, but most importantly, use your instincts to decide which activities may be most appropriate for your child.

LET'S START COUNTING

Believe it or not, oodles and caboodles of numbers are all around you everyday. You may be surprised when you discover them at snacktime, while singing songs, and taking nature walks. Ahead are plenty of fun games you can enjoy indoors, outside — even in bed! So get ready to shout, jump, and sing as you count 1-2-3!

Ready, One, Two, Three!

Jumping and clapping are fun for me,
Especially when I count to three.

1 Ask someone else to count to 3 out loud and say a word like jump, clap, hug, giggle, sneeze, spin, smile, roll, or yawn, right after.

2 Do what the other person says 3 times.

3 Switch places. Now it's your turn to count to 3 out loud and say "jump" or "clap."

MORE NUMBER FUN

- Think of other things you can do after counting to 3 such as roll *under* the table, run *around* the yard, or jump *over* your teddy bear. How about step *over* the dog or stand *in* the laundry basket?

- Ask a friend to roll 2 dice. Then, count the number of dots, and call out something to do that many times: somersaults, mini sandwich bites, jumping jacks.

- Make a rhyme by counting to 3 and calling out an action that rhymes with the last number you called out. Then, do that thing 3 times: *One, two, three — touch my knee!; One, two, three — drink some tea!; One, two, three — buzz like a bee!*

1 · 2 · 3 Drink some tea!

HELPING LITTLE HANDS

These activities will help children learn to listen to others, follow directions, move independently, and understand spatial relationships.

Practicing these activities can prepare your child for help around the house, such as picking up things, feeding a pet, or even helping you as you follow a recipe for baking chocolate chip cookies.

Noisy Animals

Count to three, that is all you do,
Say quack! quack! quack! or moo! moo! moo!

1 Count to 3 and say the name of an animal or bird, like a duck.

2 Imitate the sound of a loud duck 3 times — quack! quack! quack!

3 Play with a friend, taking turns naming an animal and then making its sound together 3 times. You'll have one noisy farm or zoo!

1 2 3

QUACK! QUACK! QUACK!

Prowl Around

Sounds aren't the only way we can tell if an animal, bird, or vehicle is around — we can tell by the sights and smells around us, too.

Go on a wildlife prowl and look for evidence of animals and birds. Do you see a nest in a tree? Droppings in the snow? Paw prints in the mud? How would you know if a skunk was around?

MORE NUMBER FUN

● Think of 3 animals you would find on a farm and count them on your fingers as you say their names out loud.

Now count and name 3 animals you could see at the park. What might you see at the ocean?

HELPING LITTLE HANDS

If your child finds other sounds more interesting, suggest using those they might hear around the home or neighborhood, such as a vacuum cleaner, a clock, and purring cat, or a car, a train, and a fire engine.

Kitchen Fun

Pouring, measuring, watering, too,
Wet kitchen fun is in store for you.

HERE'S WHAT YOU DO

1 Mix up the measuring cups on the floor.

2 Now put the cups in order in a row, from largest to smallest.

3 Fill the middle-sized measuring cup with water. Do you think the bigger cup can hold all of the water? Do you think the smaller measuring cup can hold all of the water? Try it and see!

MORE NUMBER FUN

● Mix up 3 plastic measuring cups and 3 measuring spoons. Then, sort them into 2 piles: one pile with cups, one pile with spoons. Sort the objects by size, stacking the smallest cups and spoons inside the next larger and so on.

● Ask a grown-up if you can help make a batch of sugar cookies. Have fun measuring out different dry ingredients like flour and sugar.

HELPING LITTLE HANDS

The kitchen is a wonderful place to explore measuring and sorting, but close supervision is necessary.

Keep plastic bowls, containers, measuring spoons and cups on hand for kids to explore graduated sizes when playing in the kitchen or the bathtub.

Magic Wand

You can become a duck on a pond
With just three taps of a magic wand!

ONE ☆ TWO ☆ THREE

HERE'S WHAT YOU DO

1 Pretend that you are a magician who changes objects with the touch of your magic wand. Then, look around the room and gently tap 2 things you see that are red. What would you change those 2 red things into?

2 Now move to another room and use your wand to tap 2 things that are blue.

3 Tap 2 things that are round; then 2 things that are square.

Presto!

With just a little imagination and a paper towel tube, you can make an outstanding wand. Just wrap the tube roll with different colored ribbon or yarn. Draw designs with glue around the wand; then sprinkle on glitter or confetti for a magical, sparkling look.

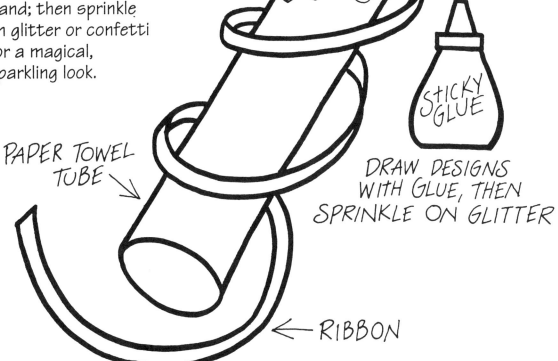

GLITTER

STICKY GLUE

DRAW DESIGNS
WITH GLUE, THEN
SPRINKLE ON GLITTER

PAPER TOWEL
TUBE

← RIBBON

MORE NUMBER FUN

● Invite a friend to join in the fun. Get your imagination rolling by "turning her into" an animal or an object. Lightly tap your friend 3 times and say "one, two, three — presto! you're a bunny rabbit." Your friend then becomes a bunny rabbit and hops around. Take turns tapping and acting.

Sing to Three!

Sing some songs from one up to three,
It's lots of fun for you and me.

1 Sing the song *Three Blind Mice*.

2 Now substitute the following words to the same tune. Hold up the right number of fingers as you sing *one, two,* and *three.*

One, two, three.
One, two, three.
See how I count,
See how I count.
I count one, two, three, and I start with one,
I count one, two, three, it's a lot of fun!
I count one, two, three, and now that I'm done,
I can count to three.
I can count to three.

MORE NUMBER FUN

● Make up other songs with one, two, three. Sing the numbers to a tune you already know or make up an entirely new song yourself! Here's one to sing to *The Farmer in the Dell*:

I love to count to three,
I love to count to three,
I start with one, my work is done,
when I say one, two, three.

● Listen to *The Thirteen Days of Halloween* by Carol Greene and listen for number words like two and three in the song. Then, sing the song along with the music.

HELPING LITTLE HANDS

Use Sing to Three to encourage auditory skills. Prompt a reluctant singer by saying the words together as a rhyme. Or, have children hum the tune while you sing.

Smile Awhile

Your face shows when you're happy or sad,
And even when you're angry or glad!

1 Name 1 thing that makes you angry.

2 Now name 2 things that make you laugh.

3 Finish by naming 3 things that make you happy.

4 Now try again, this time naming 1 thing that makes you sad, 2 things that taste terrible, and 3 sounds you like to hear.

● Here's a funny face game to play alone with a mirror or with a friend. Cover up your face with your hands; then count to three and say a feeling. You might choose "one, two, three — angry!" or "one, two, three — scared!" Now show that feeling on your face.

● Look through a magazine or extra photographs to find people displaying different feelings. Cut out the pictures and paste them to construction paper for a feelings' collage.

Funny Feelings

After you've shown a feeling using facial expressions, tell a story or draw a picture about what could make you have that feeling. Tell a story about a time when you felt happy, silly, or sad. What other things would make you feel that way?

BY ME

 Smile Awhile teaches children to identify and explore their emotions, as well as to be sensitive to the thoughts and feelings of others. Discussing feelings with children will bring you closer to understanding their likes and dislikes, too.

Clay Numbers

I love to roll and pat the clay.
It's so much fun to do all day.

I feel one and three!

HERE'S WHAT YOU NEED

Table or play area

Homemade Clay
(see page 21)

HERE'S WHAT YOU DO

1 Roll the clay back and forth with both hands, making 3 snakes.

2 Bend and curl the clay snakes to form the numbers 1, 2, and 3 in order.

3 Close your eyes while a partner moves the numbers around.

4 See if you can identify each number with your eyes closed by feeling its shape.

● Use 2 lumps of clay to make impressions from 2 different objects in the room; then have a partner guess where in the room your impression came from.

HELPING LITTLE HANDS

By providing children with manipulatives such as clay, you will help them build manual dexterity and independence in their thinking. This activity is also a good way to introduce numbers with their corresponding numerals.

Homemade Clay

You'll need a grown-up to do the cooking here, but you can do the mixing. Combine in a saucepan 1 cup (250 ml) flour, 1/2 cup (125 ml) salt, 1 cup (250 ml) water, a few drops of food coloring, 1 tablespoon (15 ml) vegetable oil, and 2 teaspoons (10 ml) cream of tartar. Cook over medium heat, stirring constantly, until a ball is formed. Let cool completely. Now YOU knead the clay until it is smooth and not sticky. This clay will last about one week when stored in an airtight plastic container or bag.

Three Party

The party's just starting,
Great times are ahead.
Join up with some bear friends,
And play on your bed!

HERE'S WHAT YOU NEED

3 small plastic cups

3 finger foods (raisins, chocolate chips, peanuts)

2 stuffed animals or dolls

1 Arrange your stuffed animals on your bed near you.

2 Put 1 cup in front of each of your stuffed animals and 1 in front of you.

3 Count how many cups you have; then place one of each different kind of food in each of the cups.

4 Spill out the treats from each cup, one at a time, counting and eating each piece of food as you go. Be sure to help the animals eat their treats, too!

MORE NUMBER FUN

● Sort out the remaining foods so that only 1 kind of food is in each cup. You may want to sort all the raisins in 1 cup and all of the peanuts in another. What other ways can you sort your foods? By color? By shape? Rough or smooth? Salty or sweet? Don't forget to eat your treat!

● Add other types of small foods to the mix; then sort the foods into muffin tins.

HELPING LITTLE HANDS

Three Party builds manual dexterity while familiarizing children with counting and sorting in a fun way. If your child is age 3 or younger, peanuts and other tiny foods may be too dangerous for swallowing. Instead, include only small foods that you know are safe for your child to eat.

LET'S COUNT HIGHER

Counting doesn't stop with 1, 2, and 3, of course. There are many other numbers yet to go! Whether you're sorting socks from the laundry basket or putting together a pretty picture collage, you'll learn plenty about numbers while playing these different games. So put on your thinking cap and get ready to count up to 10!

Sock Sort

Two socks, four socks, six socks, eight,
Matching socks can sure be great!

HERE'S WHAT YOU DO

1 Mix up the socks and spread them out on the floor.

2 Count how many socks you have.

3 Pick up one sock and find the one that matches it for a pair. Now match up the others until you've used up all the socks. How many pairs do you end up with?

MORE NUMBER FUN

● The next time someone in your family does the laundry, ask if you can sort *all* of the socks. Put all of the white socks in one pile, all of the solid colors in a second pile, and all of the socks with stripes, patterns, or designs on them in a third pile. Which type of sock do you have *most* of? Which type of sock do you have *least* of?

HELPING LITTLE HANDS

Sock Sort can be adapted easily for various skill levels. The possibilities for sorting are endless: try matching socks different in size or color for younger children, or counting them by two's for older ages. You'll soon have an expert helper for laundry day!

Sock Creatures

Tape a piece of construction paper to the table. Place 2 or 3 socks on the paper so the open end is flat against the paper's bottom edge. Draw around each sock with a crayon for sock creature outlines. Remove the socks; then glue on dried peas, beans, macaroni, and pieces of cereal on the toe ends of each sock to make faces for your creatures. Let dry.

Pretty Paper Orchard

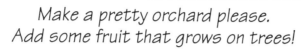

Make a pretty orchard please.
Add some fruit that grows on trees!

HERE'S WHAT YOU NEED

Colored tissue paper

Drawing paper

Eraser
(use the end of a pencil)

Crayons,
assorted colors

Glue or paste

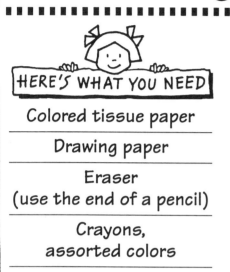

HERE'S WHAT YOU DO

1 Draw 5 trees on your paper using crayons.

2 Now think of a fruit you like to eat.

3 Tear the tissue paper into small squares. Then hold down your eraser on each square and twist the eraser, wrinkling up the paper to make fruit for your trees.

4 Glue or paste one fruit to the first tree, two to the second tree, and so on, until you have a tree with 5 fruits.

5 Write the number of fruit pieces each tree has on its trunk.

Enjoy your pretty paper orchard.

MORE NUMBER FUN

● Use different colors of tissue paper for a single silly tree with 5 different kinds of fruit!

● The next time you visit the fresh market or grocery store, look at all the different fruits. Count 5 fruits that you like, 6 that have smooth skins, 7 that are round, and 8 that are red.

HELPING LITTLE HANDS

Counting familiar objects is a good way to give numbers meaning. Pretty Paper Orchard can also lead to a conversation about different kinds of fruit, helping to build a descriptive vocabulary. Use precut tissue squares to save time when crafting.

PRICKLY PEAR

Orchard Visit

Whether you live in the city or the country, near the ocean, desert, or hills, you are sure to find trees and even cacti that bear fruit during the year. If you live where there are apple orchards or orange groves, visit these places with a grown-up for a fruit-picking trip. If you live where cacti grow, look closely at the different kinds of fruits that emerge on these thorny plants. How many different kinds of fruits grow where you live?

How Many Chirps?

CHIRP · CHIRP

CHIRP · CHIRP

CHIRP · CHIRP

CHIRP · CHIRP

CHIRP · CHIRP

Listen to chirping
Of birds in the trees.
They fly through the sky
And land where they please.

CHIRP · CHIRP

CHIRP

CHIRP

CHIRP · CHIRP

CHIRP

CHIRP · CHIRP

1 Go outside and listen very quietly for chirping birds. How would you describe the sounds you hear? High? Loud? Gentle?

2 Listen again, but this time count 10 chirps on your fingers.

MORE NUMBER FUN

● Try to count to 5, 6, or 7 between chirps.

● Count 6 different sounds you hear outdoors; then count 6 sounds you hear indoors.

● Sit outdoors and let your ears do the work. Is it very quiet or very noisy? What do you think is meant by "the sound of silence"?

Sweet Songs

Listen for different bird songs and then imitate what you hear. Chickadees, robins, and sparrows are wonderful birds that have very simple songs. You might want to listen to a recording of a bird that lives where you do; then go outside and listen for that bird's song.

HELPING LITTLE HANDS

This nature activity helps children associate sounds they hear with animals and everyday objects, while practicing their counting skills and descriptive vocabulary.

Picture Sort

Cut out some pictures of things that will float —
Include in your pile a ship and tugboat!

1 Look through magazines and find 6 pictures of boats.

2 Now find 7 pictures of vans.

3 Look for 8 truck pictures and 9 pictures of cars.

4 Cut out the pictures and sort them into 4 different piles: one for cars, one for trucks, one for boats, and one for vans.

5 Place your pictures side-by-side in a row, from smallest to largest.

Pocket Rocket

Use a tissue paper tube covered in aluminum foil to make a mini-rocket ship. Tape red, orange, or yellow streamers to the inside edge to look like flames coming out of one end.

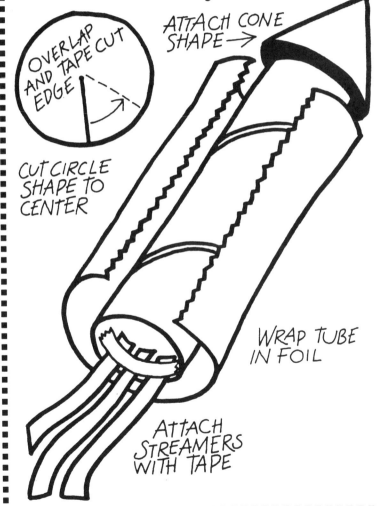

OVERLAP AND TAPE CUT EDGE

ATTACH CONE SHAPE →

CUT CIRCLE SHAPE TO CENTER

WRAP TUBE IN FOIL

ATTACH STREAMERS WITH TAPE

MORE NUMBER FUN

● Cut out pictures of planes, rockets, tractors, bulldozers, boats, and more. Sort them into piles of air, land, and water transportation.

● Look at the pictures of the cars very carefully. What do you notice about them that is alike? What do the boats all have in common? The planes?

Helping Little Hands

Learning to sort is an important first step in counting objects. Picture Sort helps kids practice sorting objects by type and size. Encourage kids to think about their own experiences when sorting by asking questions like "What else have you seen before that has 4 wheels?" or "Would you group a helicopter with cars or with airplanes?"

Six Scents

Smell some spices,
Pick the best.
Make a 6 then
Take a rest.

HERE'S WHAT YOU NEED

6 different spices

6 film canisters or other small plastic containers

Paper

Glue

HERE'S WHAT YOU DO

1 Put one spice in each canister.

2 Smell each container. How many different smells do you have?

3 Which spice is your favorite to smell? Your next favorite?

4 Put the spice canisters in order from the spice you like the most to the spice you like the least.

● Choose your favorite spice for a spicy number print. Spread glue on a sheet of paper in the shape of a number, 5 through 10. Sprinkle the spice on the glue and shake off the rest.

● Have you ever made cinnamon toast? Toast a piece of bread. Butter and then sprinkle with a mixture of sugar and cinnamon. Yum!

MY PEPPERMINT NUMBER PRINT

HELPING LITTLE HANDS

If putting the spices in order by preference is too challenging, have your child sort them into 2 groups — spices they like and spices they don't like. This is a good activity to reinforce the concept of ordinals, as you discuss each child's spice preferences.

Love You Lots

"I love you lots" is nice to say.
It means so much when shown each day.

1 Play "I love you" with a friend. You say it first.

2 Then your friend says, "I love you, two," while holding up 2 fingers.

3 Take turns saying, "I love you, three," "I love you, four," and so on, until you get all the way to ten. Be sure to hold up the number of fingers you say out loud as you count.

4 Give each other a great big hug!

● Get a package of M&Ms or jelly beans. Sort them into piles by color. Put the piles in order from most to least. Now count them to see if you guessed right. Then, for a special treat, share the candies with your friend.

Same & Different

People are both the same and different in many ways. We are all the same because we are all humans, but we're also different in many wonderful ways. Invite a friend to join you in finding 4 things about you that are the same. Now find 4 things that are *different*.

Up On Top

Climb the mountain to the top.
Take ten things and do not stop.

1 Pretend to climb a mountain as you say "I climbed to the top of a mountain and I took 1 (something)."

2 Have your friend say the same thing except take 2 of something different.

3 Now you say the same thing only this time take 3 of something. Keep taking turns with your friends until you get to 10.

I climbed to the top of a mountain and I took my blanket!

...I took one blanket and two toys!

MORE NUMBER FUN

● If you were really climbing a mountain, what 6 things might you smell? What 7 things would you hear? What are 8 things you might see? Are there 9 things you could touch on a mountain?

● Look through magazines for pictures of mountains. Then, draw a picture of a mountain reaching up to the sky.

HELPING LITTLE HANDS

Up on Top has many learning dimensions. It helps children use their imaginations, explore their senses, and strengthen their reasoning abilities. Take a real nature hike and discuss what you see, hear, smell, and feel around you.

Muffin Cup Count

How many pennies inside of each cup?
Spill out on the floor and count them all up!

HERE'S WHAT YOU NEED

7 paper muffin cups

An assortment of small items (paper clips, pebbles, cotton balls, pennies, puzzle pieces)

HERE'S WHAT YOU DO

1 Put 1 item in the first cup, 2 in the second cup, 3 in the third cup, all the way until you've filled the seventh cup.

2 Close your eyes and gently move the cups around.

3 Now open your eyes and count the items in each cup again.

4 Put the cups back in order, beginning with the 1-item cup and ending with the 7-item cup.

MORE NUMBER FUN

● Spill out all the items onto the table and make 2 piles: things that are hard and things that are soft; things that are shiny and things that are not.

HELPING LITTLE HANDS

If a child has mastered numbers 1 through 7, put more items in the muffin cups or small bowls. Once all the pieces are on the table, make up fun counting and sorting games to play with the pieces.

Sew-Up Numbers

Make some special number cards with colored index cards and pretty yarn or ribbon. Ask a grown-up to help you punch holes in the index cards in the design of a number 1 through 7. Then, use pretty string, yarn, or ribbon to "sew" through the holes, creating a pretty number on each card.

DRAW A NUMBER ON AN INDEX CARD

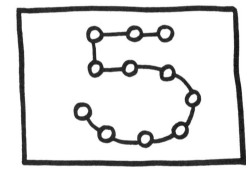

PUNCH HOLES IN THE SHAPE OF THE NUMBER

SEW THROUGH THE HOLES

Guess It

....

*Thinking of a number,
I know that you can guess.
I'll tell you if it's more,
I'll tell you if it's less.*

1 Have a friend or a grown-up write a number from 1 to 10 on a piece of paper. Don't peek!

2 Now take a guess at what the number is.

3 Your friend will tell you if your guess is correct or if the number you guessed is higher or lower than the number written down.

4 Keep guessing, using the clues your friend gives you, until you name the number.

5 Take turns thinking of numbers and guessing.

MORE NUMBER FUN

● If you're an expert guesser, try listening to these clues to figure out the correct number. What number is more than 5 but less than 7? What number is one fewer than 8 but more than 6? What number is 2 more than 6 but 3 fewer than 11?

● If you can count to 7, beginning with 1, can you count to 1 backwards, beginning with 7?

HELPING LITTLE HANDS

This game will enhance understanding of the order of numbers while using problem-solving skills. If your child has trouble determining numerical order, wait a month and try the activity again. Or, have the child use manipulatives to "see" the answer. Manipulatives and visual cues work well for children who may have difficulty with word problems. Teach them to "draw" or "construct" the word problems.

LET'S COUNT OUR FAVORITE THINGS

Each of us has favorite things we like best. You may like chocolate chip cookies, trips to the zoo, or slumber parties. Or maybe ladybugs, bulldozers, and cats are what you like most. Do you have a lucky rabbit's foot or a favorite number? Just imagine all the fun things you have yet to do or see and even taste that will make it on your list of favorite things someday.

Counting Bugs & Birds

Bugs and birds are here and there,
On the ground and in the air.

1 Ask a friend or grown-up to go for a walk with you outside.

2 First, look for 5 bugs.

3 Next, look for 6 birds.

4 Then, listen for 7 different sounds.

MORE NUMBER FUN

● Give some names to the birds and bugs you see like "creepy, crawly, green bean worm" or "the soft-as-a-pillow bird." Which bugs like to crawl? Which like to fly? When you come back from your walk, draw the birds and bugs you saw.

HELPING LITTLE HANDS

Counting Bugs & Birds invites your child to explore and appreciate the environment. Children don't need much encouragement to develop interests in bugs, birds, the environment, and animal habitats. Consider building a bird house or a bug habitat so your child can have ongoing access to the natural world.

WOOLY BOOLY WORM

CHICKY CHICKADEE

WHO ARE YOU BIRD

ITSY BITSY SPIDER

FOG HORN TOMATO WORM

BY ME

How Many More Days?

*Some days go fast,
Others go slow.
How many days
Until we go?*

HERE'S WHAT YOU NEED

A calendar that shows the days of the month

SUN	MON	TUE	WED	THUR	FRI	SAT
			1	2	3	4
5	6	7	8 ZOO	9	10	11
13	14	15	16	17	18	
	20			23	24	25
26			30	31		

HERE'S WHAT YOU DO

1 Look at the calendar and plan a special happening this month. You may want to take a trip to the zoo or the library or stay overnight at a friend's home.

2 Ask your helper to show you which square is today and how to count the squares from left to right.

3 Count the number of squares (days) you have until you reach your special day.

4 Each day, cross off a square until your special day arrives.

MORE NUMBER FUN

● Put a sticker on the square for your special day. Then, tape a penny or a pretty stone to each square on the calendar between today and your special day. Every morning help yourself to the treat that is in that day's square. When all the pennies are gone, your special day is here!

● Talk about the things you did *yesterday*. What are some of the things you will do *today*? What would you like to do *tomorrow*?

● What day of the week is today? What day is tomorrow? What day was yesterday?

My Own Calendar

Keep track of the days of the month with a giant calendar. Ask an older helper to help you draw a grid on poster paper with a square for each day of the month. That person can write the dates in each square. Draw a sun, clouds, raindrops, or snowflakes to show the weather each day.

SUN	MON	TUE	WED	THUR	FRI	SAT
1	2	3	4	5	6	7
8	9	10	11	12		

HELPING LITTLE HANDS

This activity helps kids begin an understanding of time as represented on paper. It also introduces kids to left-to-right progress — an important concept for beginning readers. For children just learning to count, keep the countdown days fewer than 10.

Balancing Hats

Balancing hats is hard to do.
I'm going to sneeze. Uh oh, ah choo!

HERE'S WHAT YOU NEED

5 hats on a bed

Take the last hat from off the bed, 5 funny hats are on my head.

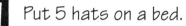

HERE'S WHAT YOU DO

1 Put 5 hats on a bed.

2 Say out loud "Pick a funny hat for me to wear, one that's so silly people will stare."

3 Then put 1 hat on your head.

4 Say "Take another hat from off the bed, 2 funny hats are on my head." Then try to balance another hat on top of the first hat on your head!

5 Repeat the poem, adding an additional hat until you have balanced all 5 hats.

6 When you've finished, say "Take the last hat from off the bed, 5 funny hats are on my head." Pretend to sneeze, knocking all the hats off!

Comic Strip Hat

All you need to make a funny hat is a 2-page section of the Sunday funny papers!

1. Fold the paper along its natural, vertical crease.

2. Fold 2 corners (the ones formed by the folded edge of the paper) toward the horizontal crease in the middle. The folded edges should be lined up with the horizontal crease.

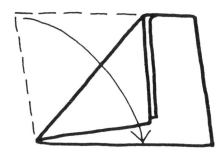

3. Fold once more along the horizontal crease to make a triangle.

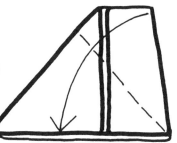

4. At the back of the hat where all the open edges are, overlap the sides and tape or paper clip together.

HELPING LITTLE HANDS

No hats? Use socks instead, putting 5 socks on different body parts: one on each arm, one on each foot, and one on your ear perhaps!

Sticks & Stones

Sticks and stones are all around,
Just stop and look upon the ground.

1 Ask a friend or grown-up to go for a walk with you.

2 Search along the ground for unusual-looking sticks and stones.

3 Find 2 each of leaves, stones, and sticks.

4 Return the sticks and stones where you found them.

MORE NUMBER FUN

- Search for 5 leaves, 6 stones, and 7 twigs. Which stone is the heaviest? Which twig is the shortest? Which leaf is the biggest?

- Think about the different kinds of things you would find if you lived in a desert. How about if you lived near the ocean? On a farm? In a city?

HELPING LITTLE HANDS

Nature activities lend themselves well to simple counting and measurements such as heaviest, shortest, and biggest. Younger children can look for 1, 2, or 3 of each thing or for pictures in magazines, while older children may want to search for up to 10 of each item for a treasure hunt.

Piggies

Counting our toes is fun to do.
You count for me, I'll count for you.

1 Take off your shoes.

2 Count all of your fingers and then count all of your toes.

3 Count your friend's fingers and toes. Do you have the same number of fingers and toes?

4 Let your friend count your fingers and toes. Does your friend have the same number of toes as you do? How about fingers?

ONE LITTLE PIGGY

TWO LITTLE PIGGIES

THREE LITTLE PIGGIES

MORE NUMBER FUN

● Find pictures of animals in magazines or in picture books. How many fingers and toes does each animal have?

● Make a collage of ears or eyes by cutting them out of old magazines and pasting close together on a piece of construction paper. Compare different ears. How are they the same? How are they *different*?

Helping Little Hands

Help your child find pictures of animals and then look for fingers and toes. Piggies will help younger children increase their body awareness, an important stage in every child's development.

SAME
2 EYES
2 EARS

DIFFERENT
BIRD'S EYE
CAT'S EYE
DOG'S EAR
MOUSE EAR

Count Around

How many things are around us each day?
Let's count all the windows next time we play.

ONE WINDOW, TWO WINDOWS ARE IN MY KITCHEN!

1 Think of something you would like to count, like the number of windows in your kitchen.

2 Guess how many windows there are in that room.

3 Now count how many windows you find there.

4 Take turns with a friend guessing and then counting different things such as chairs in your classroom, plates in a cupboard, beds in your home.

This activity helps children sharpen estimating skills and visual discrimination of objects. You may wish to give your child estimating aids such as narrowing the choice (are there 3 or 5 beds in the house?) and using clues (let's count who sleeps here every night).

MORE
NUMBER FUN

● Think of a circle. Hunt for 3 objects that have a circle shape around your home or school. Now think of a square and hunt for 3 square shapes. How about a triangle? Take turns finding 3 of each shape with a friend.

Laundry Basketball

Toss the ball right into the hole.
How many shots to make your goal?

A ball

A big laundry basket

HERE'S WHAT YOU DO

1 Decide on a goal of any number from 5 to 10.

2 Stand back a few steps and toss the ball into the basket. Count each one that goes in.

3 When you reach your goal, make a new goal and start again. Or, take turns tossing or rolling the ball with a friend.

MORE NUMBER FUN

● Try tossing the ball in different ways, such as behind your back or through your legs. Can you bounce the ball one time and make it go into the basket?

HELPING LITTLE HANDS

Laundry Basketball and other ball games reinforce eye-hand coordination. Use smaller or larger goals, according to your child's ability. Younger children will enjoy sitting on the floor and rolling the ball to a partner instead of tossing.

Tower Counter

Building a tower will make you feel good.
Use old plastic blocks or some made of wood.

Blocks

HERE'S WHAT YOU DO

1 Build a city with blocks. Start with a 1-story building with 1 block.

2 Next to the first building, stack up 2 blocks, then stack 3 blocks, and so on until you have a line of buildings with the last one being a tall skyscraper.

3 Count how many blocks you stacked in the tallest building. Now count the blocks in the shortest building.

4 Knock down all your blocks and try building one giant skyscraper using all of your blocks.

MORE NUMBER FUN

● Ask a grown-up to go on a walk with you through town or on the street where you live to find the *tallest* building. Then find the *shortest* building.

● How many floors or stories is your home, apartment, or school building? Use your blocks to build a model with the same number of floors.

Stimulate your child's analytical skills by asking questions about the structure such as "Are there 3 or 4 stories in the building?" while pointing to the block tower.

Cold Splash

Counting out ice cubes is cold you should know,
Like ice cream and rain and playing in snow.

HERE'S WHAT YOU DO

1 Place a drinking glass on the table and pass a drinking glass to a friend.

2 Drop ice cubes in the pitcher one at a time, counting them as you go.

3 How many ice cubes can you add before the water begins to overflow?

MORE NUMBER FUN

● Pour the water into the glasses. Take turns sipping and comparing liquid levels. Whose glass has more water?

● Fill a wash basin or bathtub with soapy water and drop in a coin, cork, pebble, uncooked macaroni, and a bean. Which objects float and which sink to the bottom?

HELPING LITTLE HANDS

Cold Splash encourages children to use their powers of observation, and comparative and estimation skills.

Just One More

MORE NUMBER FUN

One more than six will always be seven.
And one more than ten will make eleven.

1 Invite a friend or grown-up to think of a number from 1 to 9 and then say it out loud while holding up the same number of fingers.

2 Now you say, "Just 1 more."

3 Your friend says the number that is one more than the number you said and holds up that many fingers.

4 Take turns with your friend thinking of a number and subtracting one from it or adding one to it.

● You can say "just 1 less" or "just 2 more" and so on.

● Roll 2 dice at the same time. Then, count the dots on top of each die. Which die has more dots? Fewer dots?

HELPING LITTLE HANDS

Just One More helps kids develop a basic knowledge of numeric order as well as simple addition and subtraction skills.

LET'S HUNT FOR NUMBERS

If you like "hide and go seek" games, you'll love hunting for numbers! They can be found hiding in the strangest spots — in the kitchen, at the grocery store, even on the bus. After you play I Spy and Number Charades, you'll begin to notice all kinds of numbers around you.

Sticker Time

Place a sticker on 1, then on 2,
Then keep on going until you're through.

HERE'S WHAT YOU NEED

Construction paper

Safety scissors

Stickers
(see recipe on page 65)

HERE'S WHAT YOU DO

1 Ask a grown-up to draw the numbers 1 to 10 in giant figures on colored paper.

2 Now you cut out the numbers.

3 Decorate each number with the same number of stickers as what the number represents. For instance, decorate your number 2 with 2 stickers, and number 3 with 3 stickers.

MORE NUMBER FUN

● No stickers? Glue other things on your numbers like tiny seashells, dried pinto beans, or macaroni. Then, put the numbers in order when you are finished.

HELPING LITTLE HANDS

Sticker Time enables the child to make the connection between seeing the numeral and knowing what it means. If a child isn't interested, then you can place 2 stickers next to the numeral 2, 3 next to the 3, and let the child glue them on.

Sticker Lickers

1. Ask a grown-up to mix up 1 tablespoon (15 ml) of flavored gelatin with 2 table-spoons (25 ml) of boiling water. Now you stir until the gelatin has dissolved.

2. Brush the gelatin solution on the back of small pictures or magazine cutouts. Let dry.

3. Lick and stick where you want to put them.

Refrigerator Hunt

Look at numbers on the door,
Can you find 2, 3, and 4?

HERE'S WHAT YOU NEED

Magnetic numbers on
a refrigerator

HERE'S WHAT YOU DO

1 Put a bunch of magnetic numbers on your refrigerator.

2 Now ask a friend or grown-up to say a number from 1 to 9.

3 Now you pull off that number from the refrigerator.

4 Take turns saying numbers and pulling them off.

5 Keep going until the numbers are all gone.

MORE NUMBER FUN

● Pull off all of the magnetic numbers one at a time in order from 1 to 9.

● Mix up all of the numbers; then rearrange them in order on the refrigerator.

● Sort the numbers 1–5 on one side of the refrigerator and 6–9 on the other side.

HELPING LITTLE HANDS

By making and manipulating the magnets, children will learn the meaning of numbers through their one-to-one interaction with them, a much more enriching experience than learning by rote memorization.

Stick 'Em Up!

Make your own refrigerator magnets using cereal box cardboard cutouts in the shape of numbers. Paint the numbers with poster paint and glue on magnetic strips (found in art and craft or hardware stores). Let dry completely before using.

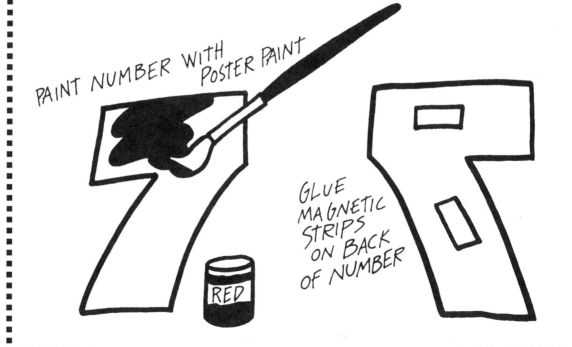

CUT NUMBER OUT OF BOX

PAINT NUMBER WITH POSTER PAINT

RED

GLUE MAGNETIC STRIPS ON BACK OF NUMBER

What Day Is Today?

I wonder the date as I lie in bed,
Yesterday's past and tomorrow's ahead.

HERE'S WHAT YOU NEED

A calendar that shows the days of the month

Paper

Markers or crayons

HERE'S WHAT YOU DO

1 Ask a grown-up to help you find today on a calendar.

2 On a sheet of paper, draw a picture of all the things you'd like to do today.

3 Now draw today's date on the paper. For instance, draw a big number 5 if today is the 5th.

4 Hang up your picture in a spot where you will see it throughout the day.

5 At the end of the day, look at the pictures you drew. Did you do all the things that you drew?

Paper Chain Countdown

Make a paper chain calendar. Pick a special day in the future such as the day you are having a friend overnight. Then make a paper chain with each chain link equalling 1 day. As each day passes, remove 1 chain link. When you get to the end, it will be your special day!

CUT PAPER INTO STRIPS

FORM STRIP INTO A LOOP, TAPE ENDS

LOOP THE LOOPS TOGETHER TO MAKE THE CHAIN

MORE NUMBER FUN

● Tell a friend or grown-up a story about something that happened yesterday. Next, make up a song or a poem about something that happened today. Then, draw a picture of something you would like to do tomorrow.

HELPING LITTLE HANDS

For older children, a fun alternative is to record events with a tape recorder. Then listen to the tape together the following day to reinforce the concept of yesterday and today.

Number Sleuth

Look for numbers where you roam,
On the road and in your home.

1 Look around your home or school, or go for a stroll with a grown-up to find the number that tells how old you are. If you are 4 years old, look all around for the number 4.

2 Look outside for your age number on car license plates, street signs, or your mailbox. Look indoors at clocks or on cereal boxes.

● In what other places can you find numbers? Look in magazines or in books for your number. How about on boxes or on cans?

● Celebrate your number by decorating your room with it. You can paint it on paper or make it out of macaroni glued to shirt cardboard.

Book of Numbers

Having your own scrapbook that shows different numbers you've learned makes a great gift for yourself. Look through old magazines to find pictures of the numbers 1 through 10. Then, cut out the pictures with numbers in them, and glue or paste each number on its own piece of construction paper. Ask a grown-up to hole punch four holes down the sides of your paper; then thread yarn through the holes to hold your book together.

PUNCH 2 HOLES →

PASTE A NUMBER PICTURE ON EACH PAGE

PUNCH 2 HOLES

TIE A BOW THROUGH EACH SET OF HOLES

MY BOOK OF NUMBERS

HELPING LITTLE HANDS

Number Sleuth encourages an awareness of how numbers are important in our daily lives. If a child is just beginning to learn numbers, focus on a single number for a week.

Whip Up a Number

Whipped topping is big fun to use.
Whip up some 4s, some 3s, and 2s.

HERE'S WHAT YOU NEED

Cookie sheet or cake pan

Whipped topping

HERE'S WHAT YOU DO

1 Spread a thin layer of whipped topping on your cookie sheet.

2 Ask a grown-up to write a number in the whipped topping. Now you write the same number next to it or trace over it with your finger.

3 Say the number you wrote out loud and then mess it up.

4 Lick your fingers and start again.

MORE NUMBER FUN

● After a grown-up has written a number in the whipped topping, trace over the number a few times with your finger; then make the number yourself — only this time make it either GREAT-BIG or teensy-tiny.

HELPING LITTLE HANDS

Tracing is a good way to help your child begin writing numerals and build eye-hand coordination. Some children may not want to put their fingers in the whipped topping; putting your fingers in first may offer reassurance.

Frosting Cookies

Number cookies are great to eat.
Count them and munch them for a treat.

HERE'S WHAT YOU NEED

Cookies or cupcakes

Frosting

HERE'S WHAT YOU DO

1 Decorate cookies or cupcakes with frosting numbers 1, 2, 3, 4, 5, 6, and 7.

2 Next, line up the cookies in order from the lowest number to the highest number.

3 How old are you? Eat the treat with your age on it now! Or, invite a friend or two to help you eat the cookies in order. Yum!

MORE NUMBER FUN

● With the cupcakes lined up in order, eat the #2 cupcake first, then the #4 cupcake second, and the #6 cupcake third.

● If you know someone who's having a birthday, decorate a cake or a bunch of cupcakes with frosting in the shape of numbers. If the birthday person is 6 years old, put a big number 6 on the cake!

HELPING LITTLE HANDS

Children love helping grown-ups with special occasions, and frosting cookies with numbers is a fun way to reinforce number recognition and numeric order, and to build eye-hand coordination.

HAPPY BIRTHDAY TO YOU!

Card Pick Up

Pick up a card and then say its name.
Keep drawing 'til the end of the game.

HERE'S WHAT YOU NEED

**Playing cards
(minus the aces, jokers,
and face cards)**

HERE'S WHAT YOU DO

1 Spread out the deck of cards and place them face up (so you can see the numbers) on the floor or table.

2 Taking turns with a friend or grown-up, pick up a card and say the number you see on it out loud. Keep each card you name.

3 When all the cards have been picked up, lay them down and play again.

Snapshot Shuffle

1. Collect 5 to 10 extra photographs of friends, family members, pets, favorite places, or other things.

2. Mix up all the photos and lay them face down in a pile.

3. Ask a grown-up or friend to choose a picture from the deck and describe the person, place, or thing in the photo without giving away the answer.

4. Now you guess what the picture is. If you guess correctly, keep the picture; otherwise return it to the pile. Take turns choosing and guessing. The person with the most pictures at the end shuffles for the next round.

MY DOG SPOT!

HELPING LITTLE HANDS

Card Pick Up helps your child recognize numbers and build memory and visual skills. For beginners, use only a few pairs. Then, as your child progresses, add more.

Card Swap

I have many cards lined up right in front of me,
Do you have a 9 to spare, or perhaps a 3?

HERE'S WHAT YOU NEED

Playing cards
(minus the aces, jokers,
and face cards)

HERE'S WHAT YOU DO

1 Take the cards 2 through 10 out of the deck and mix them up.

2 Place 4 cards face up in front of you and 4 cards in front of a friend.

3 Put the rest of the cards face up in the "draw" pile.

4 Ask your friend, "*Please give me your threes*," or any number that you want.

5 Then say "*Thank you*" when your friend passes you those cards.

6 If you have the same number to match it with, take both cards and put them in your match pile. If you don't have the same number, set it down beside the draw pile.

7 If your friend doesn't have the card you asked for, take the top card from the draw pile. If you don't have the same number, set it down beside the draw pile.

8 Take turns asking for cards and swapping them. The game is over when all the cards in the draw pile have been picked up.

● You and a friend each flip a card from the stack and whoever has the higher number keeps both cards. When you've finished the stack, count how many cards each of you has.

HELPING LITTLE HANDS

Card Swap helps children develop immediate number recognition and greater dexterity in handling thin objects, and teaches kids the importance of taking turns with others.

Matching Fun

Flip them over,
Matching cards.
Picking, pairing,
It's not hard.

HERE'S WHAT YOU NEED

20 index cards

Crayon or marker

HERE'S WHAT YOU DO

1 Make 2 piles of 10 cards.

2 Draw the numbers 1 through 10 on 10 cards so each card has its own number.

3 On the other 10 cards, draw 1 to 10 dots so each card has a different number of dots.

4 Mix up the 20 cards and place them face down on the floor or table.

5 Taking turns with a friend or grown-up, select 2 cards and place them face up in the same spot where you found them. Keep taking turns until someone has a match (a numeral card and a dot card of the same number).

6 When a match is found, remove the pair and keep playing until all the pairs are found.

MORE NUMBER FUN

● Glue 1, 2, 3, 4, and 5 different objects on cards: 1 macaroni, 2 fabric scraps, 3 cotton balls, 4 beans, and 5 pieces of ribbon or yarn. Try to determine the number of objects on each card by feeling the card carefully. When you've discovered the number, say that number out loud!

Beans!

HELPING LITTLE HANDS

Matching Fun helps children recognize numbers and associate them with amounts, while practicing concentration and tactile memory skills. For children just learning numbers and counting, play with the cards face up.

Telephone Time

Push the numbers,
Call a good friend,
Telephone fun
Will never end.

A real or toy telephone

HERE'S WHAT YOU DO

Hi! It's Me!

1 Unplug the phone. Then, put the telephone receiver to your ear and practice dialing some numbers on the phone. Pretend to call a friend or a cartoon character you know.

2 Ask a grown-up to write down the telephone number for a friend or family member. Now, plug in the phone, dial or press those numbers on the phone, and call that person.

MORE NUMBER FUN

● Practice dialing your home phone number.

● Ask a grown-up to write down the numbers you should call in an emergency somewhere near the telephone, so if there's ever an emergency you can pick up the phone and dial the numbers yourself.

HELPING LITTLE HANDS

It is good to have children practice using the phone. At first, use a play phone or better yet, unplug the real phone so the child is familiar with your home phone. Learning how to use the phone and memorizing telephone numbers helps young children feel more independent. It also can give you peace of mind when your child knows some basic safety rules and information, such as his or her name, address, telephone number, and how to dial 9-1-1 in case of emergency.

Pretty Puppet Party

*Making puppets is fun, you know.
It's great to have a puppet show.*

HERE'S WHAT YOU NEED

3 small paper bags

Construction paper

Yarn

Safety scissors, paste, and markers

HERE'S WHAT YOU DO

1 Draw the numbers 1, 2, and 3 on colored paper. Now cut out the numbers.

2 Paste one number on the front of its own paper bag.

3 Decorate the bottom of each bag to look like a person, animal, or whatever you like.

4 Put on a puppet show. Introduce your number puppets to the audience in order: Here is Mr. 1, Doggy 2, and Mrs. Apple 3.

MORE NUMBER FUN

● Make funny creature puppets from paper bags. Roll a die and count the dots on the top of the die. Give your creature the same number of eyes, legs, or any other features as the number you rolled. If you roll a 3, for example, give your creature 3 eyes!

HELPING LITTLE HANDS

Encourage kids to be silly when making their puppets. Learning and creativity happen best in a warm, supportive environment. Older children may want to make more than 3 puppets or make one puppet each for 5 or 6 friends or family members using their ages for numbers to use for each puppet.

Number Charades

Take a number and act it out.
That's what this game is all about.

HERE'S WHAT YOU NEED

20 slips of paper

2 small bags

THE NUMBER BAG

THE ACTION BAG

HERE'S WHAT YOU DO

1 Invite a friend to join you in this game. Write numbers from 1 to 10 on slips of paper and place in a bag.

2 Ask a grown-up to write down 10 activities on 10 separate slips of paper. Use action words like *jump, pat your tummy, take steps like a monster,* or *hug your partner.* Put these slips in the other bag.

3 Have your friend choose a slip from the number bag. Then, you choose a piece of paper from the other bag.

4 Act out what's on the paper as many times as the number shown on the other slip of paper (like 5 jumps). Take turns choosing paper slips and acting out what's written.

MORE NUMBER FUN

● Instead of writing down things to act out, draw pictures of different objects on 10 paper strips. You could draw 1 apple on a piece of paper, 2 smiley faces on the second piece, 3 mice on the third, all the way up to 10 pictures of something on the tenth piece of paper. Then, pull a strip from the number bag and choose a slip of paper from the picture bag. Continue drawing from the picture bag until you find the same number of objects that matches the number on the slip of paper.

HELPING LITTLE HANDS

Number Charades helps children experience the fun of counting while learning to recognize numbers at random and associate them with the amounts they represent.

License Plate Game

Find a number on a car,
Soon you'll see you've travelled far.

One·Two·Three!

HERE'S WHAT YOU NEED

Someone to take you on a walk or for a drive

HERE'S WHAT YOU DO

1 The next time you're in a car or on a walk, look at the numbers on the license plates of cars on the road.

2 Look for the numbers 1 through 9 in order. When you see a 1, shout, "One!" and then "Two!" when you see a 2, all the way up to 9.

MORE NUMBER FUN

● Look for the number that is your age on billboards, mailboxes, apartment buildings, and speed limit signs.

● Keep your eyes open for different shapes along the roadside as you travel by bus or car. Find 3 circles, 4 squares, and 5 triangles.

HELPING LITTLE HANDS

This activity helps children identify numbers in their environment and practice counting from 1 to 9. For younger children, focus on a single number for the entire trip.

I Spy

I see seven,
I see two,
Find a number,
Give a clue!

I spy a three!

1 Choose a room to visit in your home or school with a friend or a grown-up.

2 Look around for numbers in the room and say, "I spy a 3" or any number you see in the room.

3 Now your friend tries to find the number you see by walking around the room. As your friend wanders, say if he or she is getting warmer (closer to the number) or colder (farther away from the number).

4 When your friend discovers the number, switch places and you take a turn.

● Give each other clues as you look for numbers, using words like *on, under, across from, above,* and so on. For instance, "I spy a 5 *on* the refrigerator," or "I spy a 7 *under* the paper," or "I spy a green 2 *across from* the cereal box on the table."

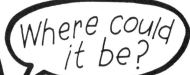

Where could it be?

HELPING LITTLE HANDS

Younger children may need some prompting with I Spy. You may want to say "I spy a 3" and then show your child a 3 by drawing it on a piece of paper.

GREAT BIG HUGE OR ITSY BITSY

Big, huge, GIGANTIC! Words like these bring enormous things to mind like castles, steamships, mountains, and elephants. Small, tiny, itsy bitsy. Do those words make you imagine mice, ants, crumbs of bread, and grains of sand? Sizing up and comparing different objects is just one good way we can learn about them.

Drinking My Milk

Milk is good,
Just drink it up.
In a glass,
Or in a cup.

HERE'S WHAT YOU NEED

Milk or other drink

2 clear glasses

1 Pour some milk or other drink into the 2 glasses, one for you and one for a friend.

2 Take a sip from your glass and then look closely at the 2 glasses. Who has more milk in the glass? Who has less milk?

3 Take turns drinking sips of milk and talking about whose glass has more milk and whose glass has less milk until both glasses are empty.

MORE NUMBER FUN

● Fill glasses with different amounts of water. Make music by tapping the glasses with a spoon. Which glass makes the *highest* sound? the *lowest*? Now put the glasses in order from *lowest* to *highest* sounds. Does more water make a higher sound or a lower sound? Create a "crystal chorus" of sound by filling the glasses with different amounts of water.

HELPING LITTLE HANDS

Drinking My Milk helps children learn about liquid volume while experimenting with milk. It's also a fun way for kids to explore sounds in a hands-on way.

Going to the Store

Going out to look and shop.
How much is that spinning top?

1 One of the best things about going to the store is unloading the groceries! Next time you go food shopping, help unload the bags when you get home.

2 Sort the items by putting small things at one end of the table or floor and large items at the other end.

MORE NUMBER FUN

● The next time you go shopping with a grown-up, look in a store window display. Look carefully at all the different sizes of objects.

● Point out the biggest thing you see. What's the smallest thing you see in the window?

CUT A SLOT IN PLASTIC LID

COFFEE

Homemade Piggy Bank

Turn an empty coffee can and its lid into a piggy bank. Ask a grown-up to
cut a slot in the plastic lid; then you decorate the can with a pig's face
and a pig's tail cut from construction paper. Or, tape a pipe cleaner tail
and some ears to the can. Search under the sofa cushion for coins and do
some extra chores for extra pennies for your piggy bank.

Bigger Is Better

Which number is the biggest of three?
Count on your fingers and you will see!

Deck of playing cards
(face cards and aces
removed)

1 Mix up the cards and then place about half the deck face down in front of you.

2 Flip 4 cards so they are face up.

3 Look at the cards carefully and say out loud which card is the highest.

4 Next, say which card is the lowest.

5 When you've guessed, turn the cards face down again and try it again with 4 new cards.

MORE NUMBER FUN

● Sort the cards into 2 piles: 1 for the red cards and 1 for the black cards. For a big challenge, sort the cards into 4 different piles according to their different black and red symbols: diamonds, hearts, clubs, and spades.

HELPING LITTLE HANDS

Making comparisons between numbers is a great way to build understanding of *greater than* and *less than.*

To reinforce the concept, try laying out refrigerator magnet numbers in order from 1 to 9 so children can gain a visual perspective on number order. If a child is having difficulty, choose a magnet numeral and count out the number of cards together.

Measure Up

Is it short, is it tall?
Fast or slow, big or small?

1 Pick a word from the following list: short, big, light, small, long, fast, heavy, tall, or slow.

2 If you picked "slow," tell a partner about something that is slow.

3 Next, have your partner think of something even slower.

4 Then, you think of the slowest thing you can. Take turns picking words from the list.

MORE NUMBER FUN

● Choose a word from the list and ask a partner to say the *opposite* word. For example, if you pick *fast*, then the other person would say *slow*.

● Use a ruler to measure different objects. Hold it next to different objects. Is a toaster longer than the ruler? Is a coffee mug shorter than the ruler? Try lots of different objects.

● Make a wet footprint mural on the sidewalk or driveway. You and your friends wet the bottoms of your feet and line up your prints from the shortest footprints to the longest.

Growing By Leaps & Bounds

Ask a grown-up to put masking tape from the floor to the top of the door sill. On the first day of each month, measure how tall you are and draw a line on the masking tape. Be sure to ask someone to write the date and your age next to each line. Then at the end of the year you can see how much you've grown!

JUNE

DECEMBER

HELPING LITTLE HANDS

Sizing different objects around the house helps children learn about the ways things can be measured and described. Give early learners a visual example if needed (the refrigerator is *tall*, the coffee table is *short*, the TV antenna is *long*).

Opposites Grab Bag

Pick an object from the sack.
Is it soft or big or black?

Several blunt objects of different sizes, shapes, and textures

Pillowcase

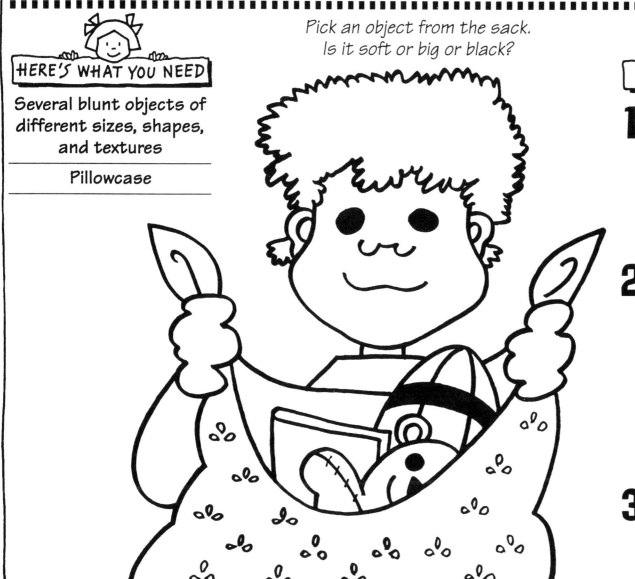

1 Place all the objects in the pillowcase: one thing that is small, one that is large, one soft, one hard, one smooth, and one thing that is rough.

2 Pick an item from the bag without looking inside it. If you picked something large, reach back in and pick an object that is the opposite, or small. If you picked something hard, try to pick something that is soft.

3 Continue picking items from the bag until there is nothing left in it.

Slinky!

MORE NUMBER FUN

● Can you tell what something is without looking at it? Ask a partner to place several new items in the pillowcase and then try to guess what each object is by feeling it.

HELPING LITTLE HANDS

Opposites Grab Bag is a fun, tactile way to learn about size, shape, and texture. If children are reluctant to put their hands inside the bag, let them look inside the bag first before reaching in.

Stepping Out

You start far apart, in distant lands,
Meet in the middle and then shake hands.

HERE'S WHAT YOU NEED

A large, open play area

A friend

HERE'S WHAT YOU DO

1 Stand back to back with your friend.

2 Now each of you take 3 steps away from where you are standing and then turn around and face each other. Are you *nearer to* or *farther from* your friend?

3 Now, each of you take 1 step toward each other. Are you *nearer* or *farther* away now?

MORE NUMBER FUN

● Which room in your home is nearest the kitchen? The farthest? Which chair in your classroom is nearest the door? Which is farthest from where you hang your coat?

● Have a near-far race. Place 2 groups of items across the room (a ball, a bat, a sweater, a hat, and a mitten). On the word "*Go,*" you and a partner each run to your pile that is far away and return to home base (near). Run for each item without stopping, picking only one item at a time. Who can bring all the far items back fastest? When you are done, play again — only this time you have to jump all the way!

HELPING LITTLE HANDS

Stepping Out introduces children to concepts of near and far/space and distance through active learning.

Sand Castle

Build a castle out of sand.
Think of knights in far-off lands.

Sand or fine, dry,
powdery dirt

Water

3 different-sized tall,
round containers
(coffee can, sand pail,
frosting container)

1 Fill 3 different-sized
containers with sand
or fine dirt.

2 Add just enough water
to make the sand or
dirt stick together.

3 Turn the cans upside
down to form the 3
towers of a castle.

4 Use the different-sized
containers to make
small, medium, and
large towers and walls
around your kingdom.

Toothpick Flags

Cut out triangles from construction paper and wrap the edge of each triangle around a toothpick. Tape in place. Then, place the flags atop the various towers of your castle.

CUT TRIANGLES FROM PAPER

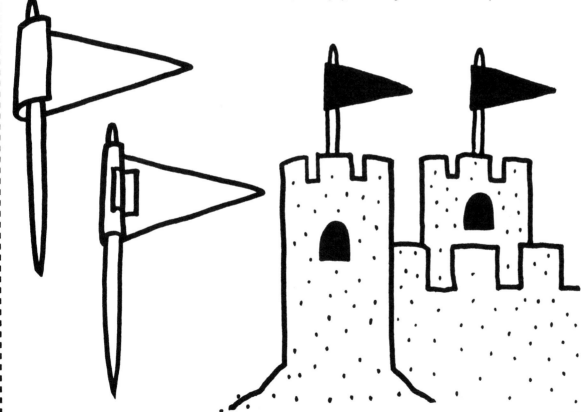

HELPING LITTLE HANDS

Sand Castle encourages children to explore various sizes and measures. This activity can be adapted for inside play by using different-sized cylinders of construction paper, taped together. Children can even color or draw details on the paper before taping into cylinders.

Lunch Time Shapes

Tuna sandwiches, I have found,
Are better when they're square or round!

HERE'S WHAT YOU NEED

Your favorite sandwich

Cookie cutters in geometric shapes

HERE'S WHAT YOU DO

1 Ask a grown-up to help you cut a shape from your sandwich (circle, square, or triangle) with a cookie cutter.

2 What is the shape of your sandwich cutout?

3 Eat up that yummy shape; then use another cookie cutter to cut your sandwich into another shape.

MORE NUMBER FUN

● Celebrate a shape with a shape meal! For circle day, eat round or circular foods like oranges, English muffins, and round cookies. Or, for triangle day, eat a slice of pizza, tortilla chips, cheese nips, and sandwiches cut at an angle!

HELPING LITTLE HANDS

Lunch Time Shapes prompts visual and memory-building skills and is an activity that travels well. Make several sandwiches at once and cut them into different shapes ahead of time so your child can compare various shapes.

Making My Shapes Book

I know some shapes,
Just take a look.
I've put them in
My great shapes book.

HERE'S WHAT YOU NEED

3 sheets of colored construction paper

Magazines to cut up

Nontoxic paste or glue

Safety scissors

HERE'S WHAT YOU DO

1 Ask a grown-up to help you label the 3 sheets with these shape names: circle, square, triangle.

2 Look for circles, squares, and triangles in magazines and cut them out.

3 Paste the circles to your circle page.

4 Next, paste the squares to your square page.

5 Then, paste the triangles to your triangle page.

6 Punch holes on the left side of each page and weave some yarn through the holes to bind your shapes book.

● Cut out different-sized shapes from colored construction paper and paste them onto the shape sheet that matches. Cut out small, medium, and large circles, squares, and triangles.

● Make a cover for your shape book from heavy construction paper. Be sure to draw your favorite shapes on it.

HELPING LITTLE HANDS

To reinforce shape recognition, have children trace over each shape with a finger. For advanced learners, ask each child to put 2 triangles on the triangle page, 3 squares on the square page, and 4 circles on the circle page.

Shape Art

Make a boat out on the sea,
Shapes are fun for you and me.

HERE'S WHAT YOU NEED

Construction paper,
assorted colors

Safety scissors

Markers

HERE'S WHAT YOU DO

1 Ask a grown-up to draw lots of different shapes on construction paper. Then you trace over each one with your finger.

2 Cut out each shape and name them.

3 Set the shapes on a table and move them around to make different pictures. You might want to use triangles to make a picture of a sailboat, or use squares for a school, or use circles for a snowperson.

MORE NUMBER FUN

● Make a great poster by pasting your best shape picture on a big piece of construction paper. Hang on your bedroom wall or on the refrigerator.

● Use your shapes to make a pattern on the table or floor. Try arranging a square-circle-square-circle pattern or a triangle-circle-triangle-circle pattern.

HELPING LITTLE HANDS

If your child is just beginning to learn to draw and use safety scissors, try drawing the shapes ahead of time and beginning the cutting yourself to get your child started.

Shape Match

Match the circle or the square.
Cards the same will make a pair.

12 blank cards

Crayons

1 Ask a grown-up to draw these shapes on the 12 cards (2 circles, 2 squares, 2 rectangles, 2 diamonds, 2 triangles and 2 ovals).

2 Mix up the cards and spread them out face down.

3 Turn over one card and name the shape.

4 Then, turn over another card and name the shape you see drawn on it. Pick up both cards if they match and put them in a pile. Turn the 2 cards back over if they don't match.

5 Continue flipping 2 cards at a time until all the cards are matched.

MORE NUMBER FUN

● Sort the shapes into 3 piles — one for triangles, one for circles, and one for squares.

● Here's a challenge: Ask a grown-up to draw the shapes on 24 cards, but this time with 2 large and 2 small of each shape. Try to match both the shape and the size.

HELPING LITTLE HANDS

Shape Match helps children build confidence in recognizing shapes while giving them practice using their memory and concentration. These are valuable pre-math skills that help children master more difficult math concepts, such as addition and subtraction.

Sand Shapes

Make a shape with lots of sand,
Use some color, make it grand.

HERE'S WHAT YOU NEED

Sand or glitter

White craft glue

Construction paper,
any color

Pen or pencil

HERE'S WHAT YOU DO

1 Ask a grown-up to draw 6 shapes on the construction paper.

2 Now you outline each shape with glue.

3 Sprinkle on the sand or glitter.

4 When the glue dries, tilt your paper so the extra sand or glitter falls off onto your work space.

MORE NUMBER FUN

● Fill a baking pan with enough sugar to just cover the bottom. Then, draw shapes in the sugar with your finger. What is your favorite shape to draw?

Texture Touch

Add small amounts of sand or salt to tempera paint and use to make an unusual texture painting. Do you feel the grainy texture on your fingers?

TEMPERA

Clay Play

Here's a game that you can play,
Making snake shapes out of clay.

Modeling clay or salt dough

Plastic knife

1 Smooth and flatten the clay.

2 Cut out a circle from the clay. Now, cut out a square.

3 Roll the clay into long snake shapes.

4 Then, shape snakes into a circle, a square, and a triangle.

MORE NUMBER FUN

● Roll out several different lengths of clay for snake shapes; then place them in order from the shortest snake to the longest snake.

● Make a special pin to wear by cutting out dough shapes with cookie cutters. Paint with tempera and let the dough dry completely. Glue on a pin.

HELPING LITTLE HANDS

Clay Play is a wonderful activity for all children, especially those who learn best through exploring with their hands.

Silly Sculpture

If you're like many artists, you love creating things that are silly and outrageous. Look at your clay and imagine something silly. Do you see a cow in a tree? A slithering snake twisting around a rock? Mold your clay into whatever shapes you see waiting to be discovered!

Mooo!

Mirror Mirror

*Say the name of a shape,
Now draw it in the air;
Use your pointer finger,
To draw a great big square.*

1 You and your friend face each other and decide who will be the leader and who will act like the mirror.

2 You say the name of a shape.

3 Now, slowly draw that shape in the air. At the same time, your friend who is the mirror follows you by drawing the same shape in the air. Try to keep your fingers close together without touching.

4 Take turns naming shapes and being the mirror.

● Play Mirror Mirror with your eyes closed! First, you and your partner stand facing each other. Then both of you hold up one hand and put your pointer fingers together. Close your eyes. Move your finger to draw a shape in the air. Let your partner try to guess what shape the two of you made.

● Ask a friend or a grown-up to draw shapes or write numbers in the palm of your hand. Can you guess the number or shape drawn on your palm by the way it feels?

Who's in the Mirror?

Look in a mirror and make some funny faces. Try a happy face, a sad face, and an angry face. Talk about what you like best about your wonderful face. Is it your freckles? Your eyelashes?

HELPING LITTLE HANDS

Mirror Mirror allows children to experience shapes through the sense of touch. Encourage children to use their different senses when exploring (touching the shape, seeing the shape, and saying the name of the shape aloud).

Going on a Shape Hunt

1 Ask a friend or two to go on a shape hunt with you. Take turns being the leader as you march from room to room.

2 In each room, the leader calls out a shape, such as "circle!" and everyone runs to a circle-shaped object or design in the room.

3 Then, march to the next room and call out "square!" and everyone runs to a square object.

*Hunt for shapes here and there,
Hiding out everywhere.*

circle!

MORE NUMBER FUN

● Choose a room at home or at school to search for objects with round shapes. Look for 4 objects that are round like a circle. Then, look for 5 objects that are box-shaped like a square.

● Have a "round" treasure hunt. Look through old catalogs and magazines for round things. When you've finished, have a treasure hunt for squares or triangles.

HELPING LITTLE HANDS

If your child has difficulty finding shapes in the room at first, prompt him or her by asking questions such as "What is the shape of the saucer under the tea cup?" or "What is the shape of the picture frame?"

WHAT COMES NEXT?

Do you wake up around the same time every morning? Does your stomach say it's time for lunch at noon most days? That's because you — and everyone else, too — have familiar patterns to your days. Nature is filled with wonderful patterns, too. Look for them in the symmetrical stripes on a skunk's back and in the leaves of trees.

But patterns are not found only in nature; they can be seen in everything from architecture and art to the four seasons and the phases of the moon!

Shape Hopscotch

Hopping on shapes from here to there,
Jump from a circle to a square.

Chalk

Sidewalk or driveway to play Hopscotch

Circle, triangle, and a square...

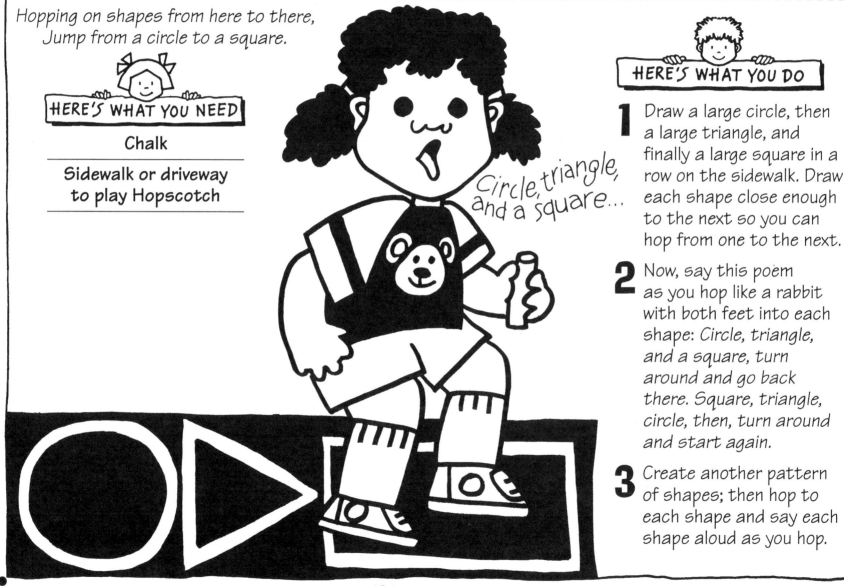

1 Draw a large circle, then a large triangle, and finally a large square in a row on the sidewalk. Draw each shape close enough to the next so you can hop from one to the next.

2 Now, say this poem as you hop like a rabbit with both feet into each shape: *Circle, triangle, and a square, turn around and go back there. Square, triangle, circle, then, turn around and start again.*

3 Create another pattern of shapes; then hop to each shape and say each shape aloud as you hop.

- Play Indoor Shape Hopscotch. Tape pieces of paper with shapes drawn on them to the floor or make shapes out of masking tape. Hop from one shape to the next.

- Write different numbers along the sidewalk; then have a partner shout out a number and you hop to it. Take turns calling out numbers and jumping.

- Have you ever noticed how the colors of the rainbow are always in the same order or pattern? The next time you have a rainstorm, go outside right as the clouds break and the sun comes out and look for a rainbow. Use colored chalk to draw the rainbow's colors in order on the sidewalk once it is dry.

Word Hopscotch

Here's a fun game you can play anywhere with a friend. Think of a pattern of words. You might want to choose color as your theme. Say "Blue, red, blue, red, blue,....?" Now your partner keeps the pattern going by finishing with the word that would come next. Here are a few patterns to get you started:
Big, small, big,.....?
Happy, sad, happy, sad,....?
Yellow, blue, red, yellow,....?

HeLPING LITTLe HanDS

Shape Hopscotch encourages motor skill development while learning to recognize shapes. Encouraging children to make up their own patterns (with help, if necessary) gives them creative control and prompts independent thinking.

Let's Plant a Garden

Plant some seeds and watch them grow,
Pretty patterns in a row.

HERE'S WHAT YOU NEED

2 different packets of seeds (grass, nasturtiums, and Tom Thumb lettuce work well)

Small peat pots with soil

A warm, sunny place to place your seeds

HERE'S WHAT YOU DO

1 Ask a grown-up to help you read the directions on each seed packet for preparing your pots and for planting the seeds.

2 Plant 2 of each type of seed per pot, so the 2 types alternate (grass, nasturtium, grass). Be sure to leave a little space between each seed.

3 When you've filled each pot, place them side-by-side in a sunny window.

4 Water your seeds and watch them for a week or longer until you see them begin to sprout.

5 Which kind of seeds sprout first? Do you see a pattern in how they grew? Do the sprouts alternate between 2 sizes? Is there a pattern of 2 different shapes of sprouts?

MORE NUMBER FUN

● Check your sprouting progress by marking on a calendar the day you planted the seeds. Then, mark off each day with a marker until you see something sprout. How many days does it take? Just count the squares you marked off to find out!

● Visit an outdoor community garden, a vegetable farm, or a botanical garden. Look for patterns on flowers. Do some flowers have the same number of leaves? Are some planted in row patterns? Do rows alternate between two colors?

Explore a Garden!

Many of nature's wonders may be hiding right outside your back door! Go outside and look around a garden — lift up stones and small logs or sticks and look underneath for small creatures such as snails, slugs, and bugs. No garden? Visit the park, the beach, or a backyard.

HELPING LITTLE HANDS

Encouraging children to notice patterns in their environment — in fences, window-panes, public gardens, floor tiles, and especially in nature — is an important step in their understanding of the patterns we see and experience in our daily lives.

Marching Time

Marching is fun as you will see,
Lift up your knees and count to three!

HERE'S WHAT YOU NEED

A few friends

Paper, several sheets

Marker

Tape

A safe, open area
outdoors for marching
around

one, two, three—follow me

1 On a sheet of paper, draw a #1.

2 Then, draw a #2 on another sheet and a #3 on a third sheet.

3 Ask a grown-up to tape a number to your shirt front and to the front of each friend.

4 Now, line up in a row with your numbers in order from 1–to–3. Who will go first? second? third?

5 March together around the room and say "one, two, three — follow me." Bang on pots or clap as you shout out each number.

6 Switch numbers with your friends, line up again, and march around the room with the new leader.

MORE NUMBER FUN

● Instead of clapping or banging on a drum, call out your numbers in a pattern: soft-loud-loud or loud-soft-loud.

● Create a wacky parade by doing other actions besides marching. Jump like a kangaroo or pretend to swim underwater — anything goes in this parade!

HELPING LITTLE HANDS

Marching Time teaches children basic ordinal recognition, while encouraging their cooperative skills within a group.

Cardboard Baton

With long streamers of ribbon at each end of your baton, you can make the colors fly in a parade! Use a paper towel tube or gift wrap tube as your baton; then create a pattern on the outside of the baton using glued-on ribbon, shiny stars, or confetti. Let dry. Remember to lift your baton high into the air as you march — just like a drum major in a parade!

Sporks

One thing doesn't fit,
You'll see very soon.
It could be the fork,
Or maybe the spoon.

HERE'S WHAT YOU NEED

3 plastic spoons
3 plastic forks
Paper bag

HERE'S WHAT YOU DO

1 Place the spoons and the forks in the bag. Shake up the bag to mix its contents.

2 Now, reach into the bag and pull out 3 items. Did you grab 3 objects that are the same? If you did, put them back into the bag and try again. Otherwise, talk about the one object that doesn't match the others.

3 Reach in again, and pull out the remaining 3 objects. Which object is the odd one out?

● When you visit the supermarket, take a look at the apples, the cherries, the raspberries, and the bananas. Which fruit is the odd one out? Can you think of 2 reasons why?

● Next time you sit down to eat with family or friends, look at the pattern of each place setting. Is the fork always on the left side and the spoon and knife on the right? Does your place setting look the same as the others at the table? After an evening meal, ask a grown-up if you can help set the table for breakfast.

● Look around your home or school for patterns. Do the windowpanes have a repeating pattern? How about the picket fence outside? Do the buses always line up in the same order or pattern every day? Do you see patterns in the grass after the lawn is mowed?

Pretty Placemats

Weave a patterned placemat you can use at mealtime. Cut 4 evenly spaced slits up the length of a sheet of construction paper, but do not cut through to the opposite end. Tape the edge of the paper so the cut ends are closed. Then, cut another different-colored sheet of paper into strips the long way. Weave the strips in between the slits for a 2-color pattern. Cover both sides with clear contact paper; then use as a placemat.

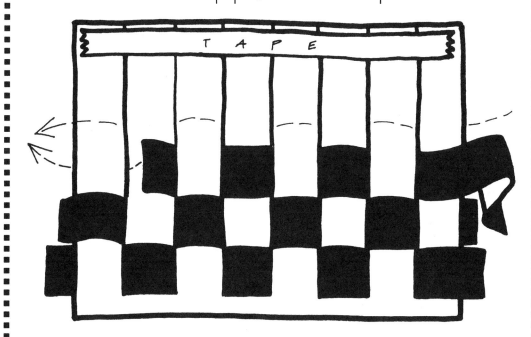

If your child has mastered Sporks, put out some flatware in a pattern on the table and let him or her select the next piece in the pattern.

Egg Line Up

Pattern skills are fun to use,
Paint some eggs with reds and blues.

HERE'S WHAT YOU NEED

12 hard-boiled eggs

Egg carton

Egg dye, 2 colors

2 bowls

HERE'S WHAT YOU DO

1 Dye 6 hard-boiled eggs one color, and 6 eggs a different color.

2 Next, make a color pattern of eggs in one row of the carton.

3 Now, have a partner copy the color pattern in the empty row with the remaining eggs.

4 Peel an egg, and sprinkle with salt for a delicious treat. Refrigerate the other eggs for snacks or deviled egg boats.

MORE NUMBER FUN

● Practice sorting other things in the egg carton such as pennies, paper clips, pebbles, shells, and acorns. Use a separate egg cup for the same types of items. Then arrange them in patterns. Your patterns can be short (pebble, penny, pebble) or long (2 pennies, 3 pebbles, 1 shell, 2 pennies, etc.).

HELPING LITTLE HANDS

Use Egg Line Up to build organizational skills and encourage flexibility in thinking, which is important for children as they grow to accept small household responsibilities.

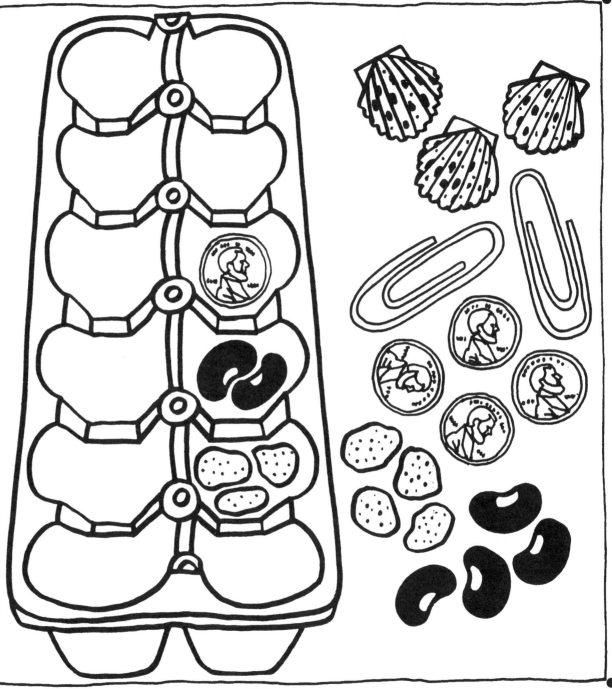

Beautiful Sounds

*Play some music high and low,
Play it fast or play it slow.*

HERE'S WHAT YOU NEED

3 glasses filled with different amounts of water or your singing voice

Spoon

1 Tap on each glass with a spoon or sing 3 musical notes.

2 Repeat the tapping or singing, but this time follow the pattern of high-low-high, or soft-loud-soft.

3 Ask your partner to repeat the sound pattern you made by tapping on the glasses or by singing the same musical notes.

4 Take turns tapping out notes or singing and then repeating what's heard.

MORE NUMBER FUN

● Sing different 2-note sound patterns with your friend. First sing high, then sing low. Ask your partner to repeat the sounds.

● Listen to the song *Row, Row, Row Your Boat* or another favorite song. Do you hear sounds or words that are repeated? Is there a pattern to the music?

HELPING LITTLE HANDS

Focusing on rhythmic sounds is a great way for children to learn about patterns in music and to learn words to favorite songs.

That Makes Sense!

Are there certain sounds you know that mean something special? What does it mean when a teapot whistles? A car horn honks? The fire-alarm rings? There are probably many sounds you know that mean something important. What does a stop sign mean? How about red lights on the street corner?

Bedtime Memories

What happened today?
You might like to know.
This morning I laughed,
Then played in the snow.

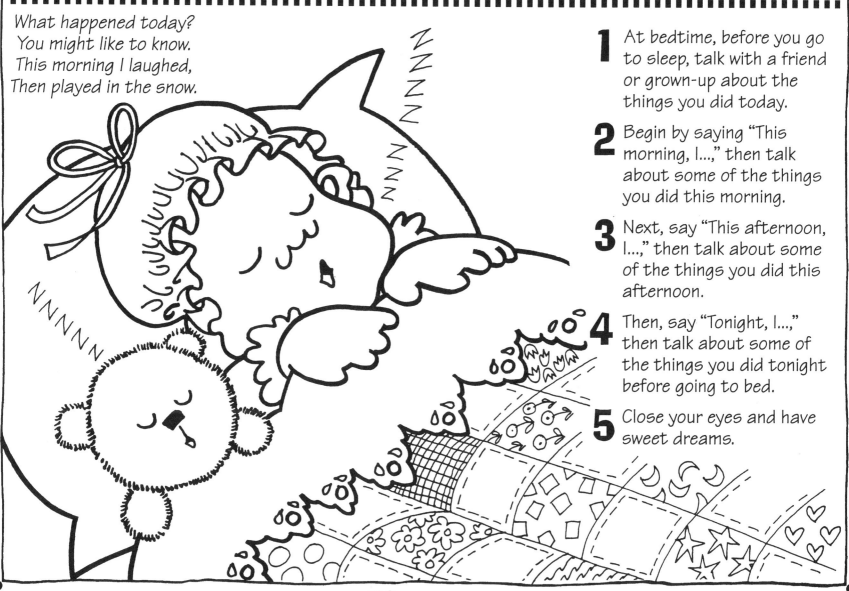

1 At bedtime, before you go to sleep, talk with a friend or grown-up about the things you did today.

2 Begin by saying "This morning, I...," then talk about some of the things you did this morning.

3 Next, say "This afternoon, I...," then talk about some of the things you did this afternoon.

4 Then, say "Tonight, I...," then talk about some of the things you did tonight before going to bed.

5 Close your eyes and have sweet dreams.

MORE NUMBER FUN

● Think about dinnertime. Which do you usually eat *first*, dinner or dessert? What do you usually do *first* thing in the morning? How about the *last* thing just before bedtime?

● While you are getting ready for bed, look through your clothes in your closet or chest of drawers. Do you have shirts that have stripes? How about floral patterns on your favorite dress? What other types of patterns do you see on your clothes? Are there patterns on your bed sheets?

HELPING LITTLE HANDS

This activity is a nice way to end the day and helps children relate the day's activities to specific times of the day, while building comfort with their daily routines.

GO TO SLEEP WHILE COUNTING SHEEP ♥ GOOD NIGHT.

INDEX

MORE GOOD BOOKS FROM WILLIAMSON PUBLISHING

Little Hands® Books
from **Williamson Publishing**

The following *Little Hands®* books for ages 2 to 6 are each 144 pages, fully illustrated, trade paper, 10 x 8, $12.95 US. To order additional copies of *Math Play!*, please see last page for ordering information. Thank you.

American Bookseller Pick of the Lists

RAINY DAY PLAY!
Explore, Create, Discover, Pretend
by Nancy Fusco Castaldo

STOP, LOOK & LISTEN
Using Your Senses from Head to Toe
by Sarah A. Williamson

Children's BOMC Main Selection

THE LITTLE HANDS ART BOOK
Exploring Arts & Crafts with 2- to 6-Year-Olds
by Judy Press

Parents' Choice Approved
Early Childhood News Directors' Choice Award

SHAPES, SIZES, & MORE SURPRISES!
A Little Hands Early Learning Book
by Mary Tomczyk

Parents' Choice Approved

The Little Hands BIG FUN Craft Book
Creative Fun for 2- to 6-Year-Olds
by Judy Press

Parents' Choice Approved

THE LITTLE HANDS NATURE BOOK
Earth, Sky Critters & More
by Nancy Fusco Castaldo

Kids Can!® is a registered trademark of Williamson Publishing.

Kids Can! Books from Williamson Publishing®

The following *Kids Can!* books for ages 4 to 10 are each 160-178 pages, fully illustrated, trade paper, 11 x 8 1/2, $12.95 US.

VROOM! VROOM!
Making 'dozers, 'copters, trucks & more
by Judy Press

MAKING COOL CRAFTS & AWESOME ART!
A Kids' Treasure Trove of Fabulous Fun
by Roberta Gould

HAND-PRINT ANIMAL ART
by Carolyn Carreiro

CUT-PAPER PLAY!
Dazzling Creations from Construction Paper
by Sandi Henry

American Bookseller Pick of the Lists
SUPER SCIENCE CONCOCTIONS
50 Mysterious Mixtures for Fabulous Fun
by Jill Frankel Hauser

Parents' Choice Gold Award
Parents Magazine Parents' Pick
THE KIDS' NATURE BOOK
365 Indoor/Outdoor Activities and Experiences
by Susan Milord

Benjamin Franklin Best Multicultural Book Award
Parents' Choice Approved
Skipping Stones Multicultural Honor Award
THE KIDS' MULTICULTURAL COOKBOOK
Food & Fun Around the World
by Deanna F. Cook

KIDS' COMPUTER CREATIONS
Using Your Computer for Art & Craft Fun
by Carol Sabbeth

Parents' Choice Approved
Dr. Toy Vacation Favorites Award
KIDS GARDEN!
The Anytime, Anyplace Guide to Sowing & Growing Fun
by Avery Hart and Paul Mantell

Winner of the Oppenheim Toy Portfolio Best Book Award
American Bookseller Pick of the Lists
THE KIDS' SCIENCE BOOK
Creative Experiences for Hands-On Fun
by Robert Hirschfeld and Nancy White

Parents' Choice Gold Award
American Bookseller Pick of the Lists
Winner of the Oppenheim Toy Portfolio Best Book Award
THE KIDS' MULTICULTURAL ART BOOK
Art & Craft Experiences from Around the World
by Alexandra M. Terzian

Parents' Choice Gold Award
Benjamin Franklin Best Juvenile Nonfiction Award
KIDS MAKE MUSIC!
Clapping and Tapping from Bach to Rock
by Avery Hart and Paul Mantell

BOREDOM BUSTERS!
The Curious Kids' Activity Book
by Avery Hart and Paul Mantell

American Bookseller Pick of the Lists
KIDS' CRAZY CONCOCTIONS
50 Mysterious Mixtures for Art & Craft Fun
by Jill Frankel Hauser

Winner of the Oppenheim Toy Portfolio Best Book Award
Skipping Stones Nature & Ecology Honor Award
ECOART!
Earth-Friendly Art & Craft Experiences for 3- to 9-Year-Olds
by Laurie Carlson

KIDS COOK!
Fabulous Food for the Whole Family
by Sarah Williamson and Zachary Williamson

THE KIDS' WILDLIFE BOOK
Exploring Animal Worlds through Indoor/Outdoor Crafts & Experiences
by Warner Shedd

HANDS AROUND THE WORLD
365 Creative Ways to Build Cultural Awareness & Global Respect
by Susan Milord

KIDS CREATE!
Art & Craft Experiences for 3- to 9-Year-Olds
by Laurie Carlson

Parents Magazine Parents' Pick
KIDS LEARN AMERICA!
Bringing Geography to Life with People, Places, & History
by Patricia Gordon and Reed C. Snow

American Bookseller Pick of the Lists
ADVENTURES IN ART
Art & Craft Experiences for 8- to 13-Year-Olds
by Susan Milord

Other Books

from **Williamson Publishing**

Benjamin Franklin Best Juvenile Fiction Award
Parents' Choice Honor Award
Stepping Stones Multicultural Honor Award

TALES ALIVE!
Ten Multicultural Folktales with Activities
by Susan Milord
128 pages, 8 1/2 x 11
Trade paper, $15.95

Parents' Choice Approved

TALES OF THE SHIMMERING SKY
Ten Global Folktales with Activities
by Susan Milord
128 pages, 8 1/2 x 11
Trade paper, $15.95

PYRAMIDS!
50 Hands-On Activities to Experience Ancient Egypt
by Avery Hart & Paul Mantell
96 pages, 10 x 10
Trade paper, $10.95

To see what's new at Williamson and learn more about specific books, visit our website at:
http://www.williamsonbooks.com

To Order Books:

You'll find Williamson books at your favorite bookstore or order directly from Williamson Publishing. We accept Visa and MasterCard (*please include the number and expiration date*), or send check to:

Williamson Publishing Company
Church Hill Road, P.O. Box 185
Charlotte, Vermont 05445

Toll-free phone orders with credit cards:
1-800-234-8791
E-mail orders with credit cards:
order@williamsonbooks.com

Catalog request: **mail, phone, or e-mail**

Please add **$3.00** for postage for one book plus **50 cents** for each additional book. Satisfaction is guaranteed or full refund without questions or quibbles.

Prices may be slightly higher when purchased in Canada.

Kids Can!®, Little Hands®, and Tales Alive!®, are registered trademarks of Williamson Publishing.

Kaleidoscope Kids™ is a trademark of Williamson Publishing.